BECOMING A KEPT MAN:

My Journey. . .And Yours

by Melvin Mason

TWIGG

PRODUCTIONS℠

PUBLISHING

Second Edition

Becoming A Kept Man:
My Journey. . .And Yours

©*2019 Melvin Mason*

ISBN 978-1-7336815-4-4

All Bible quotations are taken from the Authorized King James version (KJV), unless otherwise noted.

Also quoted:

The Living Bible (TLB) ©1971. Tyndale House Publishers, Inc.

The Holy Bible, New Int'l Version (NIV) ©1973,1978,1984 by International Bible Society, Zondervan Publishing House.

The Holy Bible, New American Standard-Updated Edition (NASU) ©1995 by The Lockman Foundation.

Published by
Twigg Productions Publishing
Cleveland, OH 44143

http://twiggproductions.com

Printed in the United States of America

DEDICATION

To my niece, Phylecia, who encourages me;

to my friend, Rowena,

who awakened my understanding;

and Lord willing, to my future wife,

whom God will have prepared & KEPT for me.

(Proverb 19:14)

TABLE OF CONTENTS

Acknowledgements

My thanks goes out to E. B., Alex, Adam, and "Mr. Snow" for helping me process and focus to complete this (and other!) work. Also, to Adrianne, Jay, and Valerie for their consultation and encouragement in the initial drafts of this book. To Martin J., a great editor who patiently walked me through this first literary effort. Most of all, I want to say thank you to God, the Holy Spirit, who teaches me and brings to remembrance all that our Keeper has spoken.

FOREWORD

"Becoming A Kept Man" is a fascinating and beneficial read whether you are single or married. Melvin dug deep into his childhood and lifelong journey to understand what God has allowed and initiated over the years. What he came to understand was that as hard as it [can be] to accept, God has been in control. Man tries to plan his development and growth into manhood, but God orders his steps. Understanding and accepting this has helped Melvin to grasp that he has been kept by God for what God wants him to be, to experience what is best, and by faith to "press on to take hold of that for which Christ Jesus took hold of him" (Philippians 3:12).

-Lud Golz

Lud Golz has been a pastor for 50 years (including founding pastor of Fellowship Bible Church, of which Melvin was a member for 22 years), and has traveled extensively to many foreign countries on mission trips over the years. Lud has authored articles and books [including *A Call To Responsible Freedom* and *A Daily Guide To Knowing God*], some of which have been translated into foreign languages. He now focuses his time on his international radio broadcast, "Getting God's Message."

Lud has been married to Muriel for 58 years and they have four married children.

PREFACE

"She's a kept woman" is what they'd whisper. In male-dominant societies of the past, females who looked to men for financial support or gifts in exchange for sex and/or their companionship were said to be "kept." These days, they're referred to as "side pieces," or perhaps "sugar babies." Well, I've written this book to share the testimony that has recently... finally...been released from within me: the testimony of who I've become! And I've become a Kept Man. Not kept by some "cougar" as a side piece for sex, but by a divine Keeper who created me for the ultimate in companionship and intimacy.

I once heard a definition of the word "glory" that's really stuck with me through the years: Glory is *the correct estimate of [something]; the accurate representation of [something or someone]*. "Therefore whether you eat or drink, or whatsoever you do, do all to the <u>glory</u> <u>of</u> <u>God</u>" (1st Corinthians 10:31). We're all born to show forth the accurate representation of God in/through our lives, including our sexuality. And to this point, I've really hesitated to do that in the area of my celibacy. The dictionary defines celibacy (in the strictest sense) as "the state of not being married," or "abstention from sexual intercourse." In modern times, celibacy has come to attach itself not only to the understanding of not currently participating in sexual activity, but also to never having had sex, a definition originally belonging only to the word virginity! And that describes me! On the one hand, I'm proud to be able to say that I'm a virgin, especially at my age, but for most of my life I was also very ashamed.

Dr. Morris Massey, sociologist and former professor at the University of Colorado and author of *What You Are Is Where You Were When*[i], once joked that "today's definition of a virgin...is: the ugliest [kid] in sixth grade!" When I heard him say that, I laughed; then my expression grew humorless, because it dawned on me that that's what I believed about me! For decades, I have felt a stigma about being a virgin, and about still being unmarried. I felt unattractive and unwanted most of my life, so there wasn't much for me to be bragging about in the area of romance! Being celibate wasn't by choice, at least not by my choice; I didn't have some grand scheme to be "pleasing to God" (though I always want to be). But it was really a fluke of circumstance. As far as I was concerned, it was the result of being less-than-worthy of some woman's attention. But as I am now discovering, I have Someone's attention, and have had Their attention all along. They are the One who prepared, preserved, and continues to keep me, even possibly for a future significant-other.

You're probably wondering, "Is it actually possible in today's world to remain single and celibate? How difficult is it?" You need to know that some things are your responsibility, and other things are not. Some things should be within your control (mainly yourself!), most other things are out of your control. You do what you're called to do, which is surprisingly not as complex as you might think, and let your Keeper take care of whatever the rest may be. If you are taking an active interest in maintaining your abstinence and pursuing a more rewarding and purposeful life while unmarried, this book is for you! Whether you feel marginalized by friends or stigmatized by society because of your station in life, I want you to know you are not alone in your current situation, nor do you have to fear being alone in your future!

Now you may have already taken a "bite" of the proverbial apple and be asking, "Is it too late for me to be kept?" Well, there are those modern-day enthusiasts who feel they can claim "born-again virgin" status simply because they have chosen in themselves not to partake in sexual activity [anymore!] for a season, stating that they will save themselves for one significant-other to be named/found in the future. And though that concept may have some merit, born-again virginity is not the premise of this book nor of my life's story. I have never had sex, so there is nothing to renew, reclaim, or rethink. And I'm learning more and more that there are those who find themselves similarly situated, either by circumstance or by choice. But I would say that it is rarely "too late" to do the right thing (see Jeremiah 3:22). So it is my hope and prayer that the stories and principles found within these covers can be helpful and encouraging to you WHATEVER your sexual status.

Subtitling this book "My Journey...and Yours" may seem strange, but in reality this has been a journey toward realizing that what I am in life (single and celibate) happened because of where I was (in the grip of my Keeper) when (I was growing up). It is by Divine design that I've been here all along, and it's appropriate to be here (Psalm 118:23-24).   And as you journey with me, you may relate to the many struggles I dealt with, and you'll read of the insights I gained as a result. But you may also find out, even as I had to realize, that you too are actually being KEPT!

NOBODY WANTS ME

"Nobody wanted me. Not my sisters or brothers; not even my own mother loved me. The only person that *ever* loved me was Mizz MacMurray!" The words poured blandly from my mother's mouth, and they shocked and amazed me as a little boy, as much as they saddened me. And I would hear her recite the tale two or three more times in my life before she died.

My mom never felt loved or accepted by anyone; not her family, her church, not even by her own husbands. My mom was divorced from her first husband in 1952, after about ten loveless years in an essentially "arranged" marriage. I say arranged because, to hear it told, the no-longer-so-young Reverend that she married needed to have his own church and be settled down with a wife by now, in order to carry the necessary clout and political weight as a pastor in the association. So his superior innocently recommended a young woman in his own church; rather a 'plain-Jane' it was said, who was available and had never been married. That insinuated that she was a virgin (and she was), which was always preferable in those days. But my mom would tell us later, "He never really loved me. The *only* person to really show me any compassion or concern was Mizz MacMurray."

Mrs. MacMurray was an elderly African-American neighbor who at one time attended the same church as my mother, and became like a mom to her when she was a poor, young, working-class woman living in the Central  Avenue projects of Cleveland in the 1940s. And now that mom was a single parent, Mrs. Mac-Murray would sometimes watch my siblings (this was before I was born) whenever mom couldn't get home right away. Mrs. MacMurray's various and simple acts of kindness toward my mother truly brought them close. She died in the Fall of '54, and my mom was changed forever. The one and only love of her life (next to God Himself) - was gone.

And though she wasn't verbal about it, her relentless sense of isolation from the rest of the world often showed in non-verbal ways. Even in the few pictures she had of herself, she always had that look of sadness in her eyes, that air of disconnection from humanity. I remember seeing a picture of her as a young twenty-one-year-old and commenting to her that I thought she was very pretty. "I would've dated you if I could, Mom," I once said to her. "I have no concept of what pretty is," she responded. "I was always made to feel that I was ugly or the runt of the family. 'You just an ugly little thing,  ain't ya?'" she'd say, quoting her family. And

2

when it came to relationships with the opposite sex, well, there weren't any. Not really. Mom never felt the men who showed interest in her were right enough or good enough. What she more likely felt (though maybe not consciously) was that *she* was not good enough. Not *worthy* of love.

In contrast, there was only one time that I ever saw my mom truly happy and at peace with the world around her, and that was when she learned she was about to die. I will never forget that look of calm satisfaction on her face, that air of "Finally!" about her, after the doctors informed us adult kids that she was dying. Oh yes, she could have taken relatively easy steps to deal with the colon cancer; they had caught it early enough. She was *not* at Stage Four. But this was the day she had longed for and dreamed of; the day she had been waiting for almost her whole adult life - to finally be released from the cruelties and anguish of this life, and never again have to endure the pains of dealing with people and relationships! And she was not about to lose that through the persistent poking and prodding of modern medicine seeking to heal her! I even remember her confiding in me one time, after one of her brothers-in-law had successfully committed suicide, that were it not for her belief in (i.e., understanding of) God, she would have tried the same thing several times herself.

I think part of my mom's problem was that she never really knew *how* to be loved, and therefore she couldn't ask for what she needed, nor readily receive what others offered. Though she never was accused of being a cold person, I

3

didn't grow up with the "warm-fuzzies" of bear hugs and butterfly kisses - not from my mom! So often I would lean over to kiss her cheek or give her a hug, and be met with, "Aw gon' boy! Stop!", with a half-smile on her face, but the other half being a look of annoyance. Yet somehow, I felt I was loved, or at least significantly tolerated. To this day, I'm considered "the mushy brother" amongst my siblings because I'm the one initiating multiple hugs and kisses on the cheek within the family. But I will say that my oldest sister loves to tell the tale of how I would regularly call her "mama" when I was too young to even blow my own nose, and my second-oldest sister is the one who taught me butterfly kissing and this thing where you can greet close family by kissing every part of their face *except* the lips (because of course, those are reserved for your future spouse - or current love)! There were times when this sister and I would just giggle constantly as I kissed or "butterflied" her on each cheek, and then progressed to her chin, her forehead, her eyelids and ears, and finally land the finishing touch on the tip of her nose. Since we weren't getting the warmth and physical closeness from either of our parents, I think we learned to appreciate each other all the more. In recent years though, I still get the occasional knee-jerk reaction of "Aw gon' boy, get outta here" (learned from our mom) when I greet my sisters with anything longer than a hug or brief kiss on the cheek. Nowadays they just laugh and chalk it up to "that's our mushy brother."

But with the lack of verbal and physical

affection, there was always this nagging thought in my mind...that I would get every so often throughout my early childhood: I fancied that maybe I lived in a world full of robots, and I was the only <u>real</u> human being living among them. Yeah, they wanted to study me, and learn in fact how humans reacted to various kinds of interactions. "But keep the boy in the dark," I would imagine them saying to one another, "...or our experiment will be ruined!"

Then there was the feeling that maybe...what if possibly...I am *adopted*?!

At the time I was born, my mom and dad were already separated and about ready for divorce, after less than a year of marriage. They were married in July of 1956. This was a second marriage for her, and the third of many (at least 8 that my siblings can fairly determine) for my womanizing dad, another Reverend. There is very little I know about my father. I'm told he was a very mean man usually, and physically abusive, particularly towards women. My overall impression and memory of him concerning me though is that he was a "sugar daddy." He, too, never showed me verbal or physical affection, but it wasn't disheartening to me at that point, it was just "the norm." He died when I was nine years old, and he didn't come around much before then, other than our annual trip to Euclid Beach amusement park with my other siblings (<u>his</u> children), or other infrequent summertime activities. Of course, for a time, I was going with him to his storefront church on Sundays, and I would try to find a pew where I could fall asleep during the service without him noticing. He or my mom would always give me some coins to put into the offering plate, and some of that I would keep to go get penny-candy in between Sunday school and regular service.

Church was very boring to me at the time, even though my father preached with amazing stamina and fire (his favorite whooping line during his sermons was "Ain't that right about it!"); but I reveled in our time afterwards. He would treat me to lunch at Eat More's Diner next door, where I would always get a footlong hot dog and a sixteen-ounce, fruit-flavored soda, sometimes with french fries. Or on other occasions, we would go to McDonalds™ restaurant, which was a new, increasingly popular fast food chain! I would always get one hamburger and/or one cheeseburger, a small fry, and a chocolate milkshake. I remember this because I always wanted to be a part of the "almost one million hamburgers sold!"

The one and only time my dad ever spanked me was one of the last times I spent the night at his house. I must have been about 8 years old. I don't even remember why he spanked me, but I did deserve it. And boy did it hurt! The combination of my father's arm strength and his belt could be lethal. He was six-feet seven-inches tall, 300-some pounds of manhood, but he told my mom later that he was so scared of physically hurting me! It was probably more likely that he didn't want to bring down her wrath. But she let him know, "That's *your* son too. If he does something wrong, that's worthy of punishment, then you have the right to spank him."

For all of his meanness and abusiveness, my father learned to be afraid of my mother.

Nobody Wants Me

Normally, she was a timid little thing, but she knew his reputation for physical abuse, and she was not about to become one of his punching bags. On several occasions, she told us adult kids of the one time he went to hit her out of anger. She was pregnant with me at the time: "He had me by my upper arms and was about to backhand me. And I told him if he ever hit me, he'd better make sure it 'did the job', or else he'd *never* do it again! And I meant every word, too!" She said the look on his face was priceless. "I was scared to death, but I didn't let him know it." It made him stop and think. "'Aw woman, gon', he said, and he threw me on the bed with great force and walked out of the room." But she never worried about his abusing her again. Of course, it was shortly thereafter that they got divorced.

Looking back, I see a number of emotional parallels between my mother and me, all of which I acquired subliminally. She was quiet and kept her emotions to herself; so do I, though I'm learning to be freer. She considered herself unattractive, and so have I. She was timid (except when it came to protecting her kids) and believed in non-violence; she passed the same onto me, much to my dismay (I'll get to that in the next chapter). My dad was not around when I grew up; and thankfully, he wasn't around to teach me how to treat women. But because there was no man present in my life, it wasn't until I was well into adulthood that I learned many of the basics of being a man: simple grooming and hygiene, personal protection, assertiveness and confidence, and most importantly self-worth. The early years of my life were fertile ground for the Devil to wreak havoc if he had been fully allowed to. But you'll see that what might have been intended for evil, my Keeper used for good, to make me a decent man.

SHAKY FOUNDATIONS

As I said, growing up, I believed I was loved, but somehow I never felt I *belonged*. One too many punishments (and I got *a lot* of spankings!), one too few "at-a-boy's!", and never an "I love you."

I never felt supported during my 'tween and teenaged years. Mom never came to, nor expressed interest in, any of my extracurricular activities, not that I was involved in very much at all. I wasn't athletic or involved in any math or science clubs, so there were no sporting or academic competitions for her to attend. About the only thing I was regularly involved in was marching band. We played primarily for my high school's football games, pep rallies, and occasionally a basketball game. But if I weren't a part of the presentation, even I wouldn't be at those functions because I'm not a sports fan. There were two or three week-long camping getaways that she sent me to in my youth, but no need to come for a visit during those short stints. I imagine if I had been more familiar with the kind of home life known by other children in traditional nuclear families I might have felt neglected and heartbroken. But for me, it was just another day in the life.

I grew up during the era of Dr. Martin Luther King Jr. and Mahatma Gandhi and their advocacy of non-violence, which my mother proceeded to drill into me. She told me, when I'm confronted, "Don't fight! But if you have to

Shaky Foundations

fight, *don't* throw the first punch," whereas a man might have said, "hit 'em first!" or "don't lose!" Not that I had a brother or uncle around to show me how to box or defend myself in the first place. "Just walk away," she would often emphasize. I can remember as early as six or seven years old being chased down the street by the neighborhood bullies, Terry and Jerry. They were brothers, and to look at them they kind of reminded me of Abbott & Costello - one short (but he was "the brains"), and one tall and thin (he was "the brawn"). They weren't necessarily buff and tough, but together as a team they terrorized most of the younger neighborhood kids like me. To this day, I still carry the knee scar I received after trying to run from their abuse, only to fall onto the glass milk jug I was bringing home from the corner store. That cost me about 10 stitches!

And bullying didn't just happen to me in the neighborhood either. It also happened at school. All throughout elementary and junior high school, I was the school "punching bag." And teachers were no help. The best I could do was to hide out in the school until most of the kids decided to go home, or else be the first one out the door, running all the way home. Neither of these worked very well, and I was constantly under attack. That whole "Don't fight" philosophy was not working. Being "the big kid who doesn't fight back" only made me the best target for others who didn't want to become the school punching bag themselves! If other timid kids could beat me (with everybody watching), then there was a good reason for other known bullies to leave *them* alone.

Shaky Foundations

Even my own friends felt it necessary to abuse me occasionally just to keep the bullies off their back! Anthony was one of my "best friends" in 5th or 6th grade. One day, unbeknownst to me, he decided it was necessary to use me to keep certain potential bullies off his back. He as much as told me this before he jumped me right on Cedar Ave (a main street). Not very many kids had gathered around as they usually might when there's a fight, but he proceeded anyway (I guess in the hope that the right eyes would see). At that point I thought to myself, "Enough is enough! This is supposed to be my friend; and he's doing this?!" So while he sat on me, punching me in the face and chest with my back to the ground, I reached around his neck with my legs (you tend to be very limber when you're young) and pulled him off of me, at least long enough to get up and run (punching him back a couple of times with my weak, untrained fists before I left).

Romance was another shaky area in my youth. Valentine's Day and Sweetest Day were big doin's when I was in elementary school. Preparing our cards and candies, making a list of whom we would ask to "be my valentine," really got the serotonin and endorphins flowing! Unfortunately, while I was busy fawning over what I considered to be "the cute girls," I was not the only one feeling the sting of Cupid's arrow. Several, shall we say, not-so-cute girls (my peers and I would say "dogs") were on the hunt -- for me! And as needy as I was at the time, they seemed even more needy than me, and I wanted to have nothing to do with them! They would slip me notes in class or try to talk to me in the halls, but I would seek to get away as quickly as possible. They were unkempt, shy, mumbly-mouthed (just like me), and in some cases probably even clinically depressed. These were usually the females whose self-esteem was as low (or lower) than my own. Yes, children had self-esteem issues in those days, even at such a young age. And in retrospect, I would imagine that my attitude toward those young lasses only contributed to their problem! Why these girls wanted the likes of me I still don't know or understand. All I know is that I wanted to be as far away from them as possible! To even be seen hangin' out with "those girls" usually meant a social death sentence, which I wasn't too far from already! Had I been smart enough then, I would have realized that they were like mirrors for me; I also would have recognized that theirs was an unspoken proclamation that, in reality, I *was* "attractive" …to somebody.

I don't remember any specific details of when females were interested in me, other than my next-door neighbor when I was about eleven years old. Barbara was not ugly, but not particularly attractive either. She was a caramel-skinned, nappy-headed girl whose body had not yet begun to blossom. Oh, but when her hormones did begin to kick in, any boy in pants was her prey. Unfortunately she, too, suffered from low self-esteem, and it was at that time I began to understand what that even meant by the way she carried herself around us guy-friends. Mike, Randolph, Barbara and I all lived near each other on East 85th St, and we always played and hung out together during those years. And it was all innocent enough until puberty hit! Then, one after another, Barbara grew a crush on each of us, and would give herself to - oh, let me just say it - she was easy! Not that any of us knew anything about "going all the way," but we did know how to play "Doctor" and "House" with all the gratuitous groping attached.

I remember one day, the four of us were in my backyard garage with the garage doors closed -- "exploring." We were taking turns fiddling about, and I was getting dangerously close to doing something regretful. My mom became suspicious at the sound-of-silence coming from an otherwise boisterous group, and called out, "I know what you kids are doing in there!", to which we replied, "We ain't doin' nothin!" Randolph and Mike then opened the garage doors enough to run out and down the street a little way, while Barbara and I sheepishly came out and stayed in the backyard, pretending to rough-house around. At one point she was over me, and had me pinned on the ground, and we were both laughing so hard that the peppermint she was sucking on fell out of her mouth and onto mine, along with a nice gob of spittle! Gack!! "Let me up, Barbara! Let me up!!" And I threw her off of me and ran into the house to wash my mouth out. Whatever sexual itch we were feeling to that point was not about to get scratched after that! The mood was gone; killed! And it was a long time before she and I could ever look each other comfortably in the face. This only added to the rejection that I'm sure she regularly felt from her stern mom and absentee dad, as well as from any would-be love interests. Not too long after that, she and her mom moved away.

But why was it that I always seemed to be "kept" from getting past second base with a girl? I think it was situations like these that created and fed my inhibitions about pursuing women on my own in the first place. The ones I wanted didn't want me, and the ones who wanted me I wasn't interested in. Besides, I wouldn't know what to "do" with them if I did catch one! I had no training! No male role models, only plenty of over-produced, un-utilized hormones. This only increased my social anxiety and sense of inadequacy in the romantic arena. But were these self-esteem issues also unwittingly doing me good by keeping me abstinent?

The biggest and best glimmer of hope in my otherwise miserable young life (though I didn't quite recognize it at the time) was my mom's pastor and friend, Rev. E. V. Hill Sr. That man spoke life into me AND over me like I had never experienced before nor since. He would regularly tell my mother, "Ida, this boy is gon' make you proud one day. He's gonna be a good young man when he grows up; he already is! You watch." And he would look down into my 6-7-8-year-old eyes, lay his hand on my head as if to bless me,  and smile. I wish I could remember exactly the things he would say to me; but all I know is I would come away from shaking his hand after service each Sunday feeling like I was a good boy in line for becoming a great man! In retrospect, I think he was prophesying over me, either intentionally or unintentionally, and I felt cared for, comforted, and loved.

By the time I was twelve, I began to take the call of Christianity more seriously. Being raised in a Christian home had no small influence, of course, and I knew I did not want to burn in Hell. So one fine Sunday morning, I decided to go forward to "join the church" during the alter call. As I stood up to walk down the aisle, my mother stopped me; she had me wait till she could confirm my sincerity. So once we were home, she asked me several questions to verify that I understood what it meant to become a Christian. For me, the motivation was actually more about having "fire insurance" (as I like to refer to it). But once I was able to show her that I "got it" (and I did, for the most part), I was able to join the next Sunday and, within the same month, be baptized. It wouldn't be until several years later that I would come to understand the <u>personal</u> <u>relationship</u> that is meant to be had with and through Jesus Christ. But nonetheless this action was the beginning of being "kept" for a grander design than I could imagine! My young life to this point was filled with sadness and various rejections that could have overwhelmed many a mind. The foundation of my life had been steadily built with disappointments, despair, and disillusionment. But at twelve years old I was at the start of a lifelong journey with my Keeper, and He was my only solid rock in an otherwise shaky foundation.

III

What's Wrong With Me!

Do you see the pattern of the Enemy so far? The subliminal message was "Nobody wants me": not my dad, not my friends, not my neighborhood. Only tolerated by my mother, shunned by the "cute girls," bullied by my fellow students. This is how I saw Life happening **to** me - dumping **on** me. For the longest time, I believed and felt I was powerless to do anything but accept whatever Life would dish out, and just hope that it wouldn't deliver anything too horrible for me to handle. Believe me, loneliness and rejection were horrible enough!

All of these things in my life helped convince me that I was not lovable, not attractive, not strong, and not worthy. "Ambition" was not a word defined in my otherwise large vocabulary, and to this day I can't stand a "challenge," though I'm told that ambitiousness and taking on challenges are generally understood to be standard character-istics of a functional male, according to divine criteria. "Men, you are called to be the protectors, the hunter-gatherers…" my pastor once preached concerning godly gender roles. But I didn't even like arguing (not that many people do) or the challenge of debate, and I would run from most forms of apologetics just so I didn't have to be the one carrying an opposing position; that would only put me in a spot to feel rejected once again. It all just struck me as…painful, or a reminder of my emotionally-painful past.

As a latch-key kid[ii], my main influences early in life came from what I saw on television. I learned how to think, talk, and try to make sense of the world around me by the shows I watched. Even now, I'm so entertained by *The Big Bang Theory* because I see so much of who I was (and in some cases, maybe still am) in each of the male characters. I can relate to and identify with many of their quirks and fears, whether it's extremely shy and clueless Raj's completely inappropriate statements to or about women; or non-athletic Howard's "mama's boy" behavior; or obsessive-compulsive Sheldon's need to always be right; or chameleon-like Leonard's willingness to do or be anything to have a girlfriend and be liked by others! Though I'd like to think I've grown out of my youthful nerdiness to a great degree, I didn't realize how much of a geek I really was until recently. In my 20s, I remember it irritated me when I thought about such weird individuals because often the ones I encountered were not necessarily interested in adjusting to the norms of society. If anything, they wanted society to see them as normal already, or at the very least, to accept them as they were. Like the characters of *The Big Bang Theory*, many real-life nerds are pregnant with potential to be serious contributors to society. In the TV show, Raj is an astro-physicist, Howard is an astronaut and mechanical engineer, Sheldon is a savant physics genius, and Leonard is a physics professor. What's more, the women on the show include a micro-biologist and a research neuro-chemist! I can tell you that, though I've grown significantly, flashes of my former nerdiness will still surface from time to time. I too have yet to attain my full potential, but unlike in my youth, I am now choosing to pursue it.

I remember realizing when I was a young teenager that I did a great deal of self-talk, especially when it came to arguing with my mother. I would finish most arguments in my head, imagining the other person's contentions and my comebacks, even if I would lose the argument (which <u>did</u> happen on occasion)! And for the longest time, I thought that I was the only one in the world who engaged in this practice (a throw-back to my delusion of living in a robot world). It wasn't until well into my adulthood that I even learned the word "self-talk" and what it means, and that all people do this to one degree or another!

It was in my teenaged years, at the tender age of 13, that I began to bring my vigorous discussions out of my head and onto paper, in the form of poetry. I discovered that I had a knack for poetry, and for writing in general. I loved the art form of poetry, especially when I learned that every line or paragraph didn't always have to rhyme. And I became a prolific writer, both in letters and in verse, though the latter was my primary outlet-of-choice at the time. It was through writing that I could say all that I wanted to communicate - clearly, fully, and tactfully - without interruption, and without rejection. No one to invalidate my feelings or convictions. It was through poetry that I proclaimed my angst about bullying, and my confusions in romance.

And ooh, the poems that I wrote. I wish

that I could share some of them with you here, but unfortunately, they were loaned to a friend who ended up losing the original works forever. Only two pieces remain: one was a word that I *thought* I originated, and the other was a poem made into a song before it was lost. The word was "cupidity," the combination of two other words, stupidity and Cupid, and the definition I gave it was "...the excessive desire for love that manifests itself through ridiculous actions or behavior. The state in which one acts like a fool for love." *[This only begins to describe me as a teenager. In retrospect, I was obsessed with the need for a female-someone to love me.]* It was only a few years later that I discovered that the word that I thought I created was actually already in the dictionary, and the established definition was already very close to what I intended mine to be: "eager, inordinate or strong desire for; lust."

The poem that became a song? Well, it's one of the first poems I'd ever written, entitled "That's the Way I Am With Love" [iii]:

Frenzied to the point of extremity,
that's the way I am with love.
Never knowing what to say or do next,
that's the way I am with love.
Lost in a daze of time and space,
never getting down to business
until it's too late;
that's the way I am with love.
The feeling is good when I first start out,
that's the way I am with love.
But as I linger, I'm then left out.
But that's the way I am with love.
And when I see

What's Wrong With Me!

that it's too late to try out,
that's when you see me down and out.
But that's the way I am with love.
As I look toward the future,
I see a glim view
of me at seventeen with nothing to do. [iv]
I look to a Person Who's up above,
and ask for help with the one I love.
But nothing happens as you can see,
it's almost as if He didn't want it to be.
But that's the way I am with love.

Even the resulting song (years later) had a sad and lonely (Blues) musical tone to it, which complemented my literary lamentation over what's wrong with me.

One of my running buddies in the neighborhood at that time was Ronald. Ronald had, among other things, a fanciful imagination. He was one who, like his older sister, really got into watching (i.e. vicariously living through) the soap operas on TV. One fine Fall day in 1970, I received a phone call from Ronald telling me of a girl at his junior high school who had expressed an interest in me. Supposedly, she had been coincidentally visiting him or something (at his house on the corner of my street), and saw me from afar, and began asking him about me. Oh my! A girl, who was interested in me?! Be still my heart!

"Tell me about her," I asked Ronald. "Well, she goes to my school, she's fourteen, she's white - or at least looks white; her father is black and her mom is white - she has medium-length dark blonde hair, keen features, and freckles." Her name was Gloria Fisher, and he

What's Wrong With Me!

said that she was kind of new in town, been here for about a year and a half, and that she was from Minnesota or someplace like that. As the days went by, he would tell me of his interactions with Gloria at school. I was only thirteen, but I was <u>hungry</u> to be loved and appreciated by the opposite sex, and especially to be romantically involved! She would send me an occasional "Hi" through Ronald, and he would hound me about how much she seemed to really like me, even though we had never met face-to-face! She was kind of on the shy side, and didn't have many friends in their school, and I was instantly attracted to this nice bi-racial girl who was interested in me! Well, this went on for weeks, and I couldn't wait for the daily reports from Ronald about the latest happenings with Gloria. We would pass messages to each other through Ron, either verbally or written, but because of her strict father, we could never talk directly on the phone (he felt she was too young), nor was she allowed to visit Ronald much at his home. And when she did make it over, it always happened to be when I was away elsewhere.

It was the Holiday season that year, and this cerebral relationship had been going on for about 3-4 months when I received a disturbing phone call. It was Ronald, calling to tell me that Gloria had been in some kind of a car accident. "She died," he said. And I began to cry profusely, barely hanging-up the phone, and without saying goodbye. I was devastated! Once again, my chance at love had been denied; one in a string of recent unrequited loves. I was on my knees in the middle of my living room, my

21

face to the floor, blubbering and snotting and blaming God for taking away yet another chance at happiness. Just then, the phone rang again, and I struggled to pull myself together enough to answer it. It was Ronald calling back to see if I was alright, and to tell me, "You didn't let me finish! She did die, momentarily, but they were able to revive her with those paddle things." "So she's alive?" I asked, curious as to why he didn't volunteer that information as quickly during the first phone call. "Yeah, she'll be okay soon; but I think her parents are planning to move out of the city, back to a more country area - for safety."

My B@!!-Sh!+ meter started going off then, and after pressing him with more strategic and demanding questions, he finally confessed that it was all made-up! All of it - the girl, the notes, the accident, everything! **I had been catfished.** I asked him why he would make up something like that and play with somebody's emotions so carelessly. The only thing he could say was that he didn't think it would go as far as it did. But the even deeper question for me was, "What's wrong with me, that I allowed myself to become so emotionally invested in what turned out to be a fictitious person?" And once again, why was I being kept from knowing true love in my life?

The following year was my first year in senior high (10th grade). I was now fourteen. I was regularly asking myself (and God!) what was wrong with me. Why was I such an outsider; a loner, with very few friends and NO social life? And what is it about me that attracts homosexuals? I mean, I'm not even close to

What's Wrong With Me!

being gay; I like girls too much. The evidence was seen in my enthusiasm for noticing beautiful women on TV, in magazines, and on the streets of downtown Cleveland. My longing for looking at women and desiring to be in a relationship had started years earlier, and the obsession only grew with time. Oh yes, the library's magazine rack was often a lonely boy's best friend. Television was much tamer in those days, whereas fashion magazines were like portable art museums with their more-than-occasional nudes and scantily-clad women. Forget S.I.'s Swimsuit edition, we had the delights of Glamour, Vogue, and Harper's Bazaar year-round. And the Devil was also busy enough to drop a sex magazine or newspaper at just the "right time" on just the right public sidewalk.

And yet on several occasions, I found myself being hit on by gay men! A comment would be thrown at me as I walked by a bar, or a "Hey, you need a ride" would come from some guy driving passed me on the street. Even a drunken neighbor had the nerve to "let himself in" to my mom's home (through a back window) to hit on me while she was at work! Man, what kind of vibe was I throwing off?

Make no mistake, I was never confused about my heterosexuality, but I did feel defeated and worthless. In hindsight I realized that these incidents were just another way for Satan to check me for flaws that he could take advantage of, to overpower me as a child of God and make me feel confused or worthless as a person. Don't be fooled into thinking you might be gay just because you don't have a whole horde of admirers chasing after you. Celibacy

23

What's Wrong With Me!

does not translate into gayness just because you're maintaining (or desiring to maintain) your virginity! And <u>not</u> being hit on by the opposite sex doesn't mean we need to dip into the same sex for comfort or sexual satisfaction.

But I did unwittingly set my sights on the ultimate obsession . . . pursuing the girl that's "just out of reach."

IV

The Women I Pursued

I was 8 years old when I first concluded that I was ready and willing to be married! After all, according to the teachings of television & media at that time (and TODAY too, truth be told!), marriage was simply a matter of finding someone you liked to look at and have fun with (and vice-versa), having a ceremony, and living happily ever after. Right?? There was no consideration of finances nor future, of being a blessing to one another nor of the sharing of one's beliefs to get in the way of judgement or reason; at least, not in a child's mind. And from an early age, my preferences in women leaned toward fair skin and long hair. That's how impactful television was in my young life! Chaka Kahn or Pam Grier might have been nice, but they couldn't compare to Raquel Welch, Linda Evans, or Farrah Fawcett. It wasn't like I was enmeshed in an actual Caucasian-dominant situation somewhere, like a school or neighborhood; and yet any chance I got to be near a fair-skinned, long-haired female was an occasion for me to fall in "like."

My first crush was when I met and fell for Linda White. She was the new girl in class, and in the neighborhood: long wavy black hair (down to her shoulder blades), a very light-skinned, bi-racial girl (like Mariah Carey), not very thin but not-at-all plump, quiet, sweet...and she smiled at me. Yes, I know, it didn't take much. She smiled at me and I was hooked. We started the whole note-passing thing (as kids do), and she said she would be my "girlfriend." My first girlfriend! She lived just a few doors down from my back door, which opened to an alley that connected to her street. So we could've played together a lot by her living so close; I say, "could have" because our get-togethers weren't as often as I would have hoped, due to her parents not letting her out of the house much.

In retrospect, I think they knew (her dad in particular!) what a "hot commodity" their fair-skinned daughter was in those days (the '60s), and felt the need to protect her from excessive attention from boys, even at eight years old. Not that I was doing anything improper with her or unbecoming of a boy my age. As best I remember, we never even kissed. This was the first girl I ever fell for romantically, but she was virtually unattainable -- always just out of reach.

As I said previously, my early preferences in women leaned toward fair skin and long hair; in other words, white women, or those who looked similar. My pursuit of these females began as early as 3rd grade, but ran into adulthood. As a teenager, I remember writing once (during my more poetic phase) that I felt

"...enslaved to my Black heritage....so when I was finally able to break free from my chains, I immediately clung to the 'white-side of the fence,' and I saw that the world around me was more than just playin' in the dirt, hangin' wit da boys, and <u>playin'</u> church on Sundays! I found a real world, a place where I could be myself & not be convicted of breaking

The Women I Pursued

the Law Of Cool!" [v]

In short, in the (Christian) white man's world, I was accepted. Not threatened nor ignored; but considered, even valued.

And thus began my more conscious exploration into the white culture of America. I was a young adult in the mid to late '70s, and although racism was still alive & well, there was also an openness (at least in northern society) to learning about other cultures and ways of thinking and behaving, whether about ethnicity, or politics, or even sexual orientation. It was the heart of the Sexual Revolution, and if I couldn't get my kind of girl to be interested in me in the Black culture, I'd try to find what I was looking for -- *elsewhere*. . .

I even kept a record of the women I encountered: my "Calendrier des Mémoires d'Amour" (Memories of Love Calendar). Gloria, Jan, Anita, Valerie, Jean, Diana, and Deborah; over two dozen names appear on it, and represent my exploration into cross-cultural relationships, particularly Caucasian-American women. I felt emotionally safer with these women, more in control, and freer to be myself without feeling judged. You see, it wasn't cool among black youth to be a guy who could cry when appropriate or be in touch with his emotions. I wasn't allowed to openly enjoy volleyball and writing poetry. You know how it is. It was more macho among the fellas to be groping girls and telling sex jokes. There's no room for a nerd who loved playing with toys and music more than playing basketball or football!

But the females *outside* of the black youth culture made room for me to be me! I

The Women I Pursued

craved to be in the arms of *that* kind of woman. I didn't care about much else. What mattered was that she paid me any kind of attention, that she was kind, and that she was not an imposing personality! Jan was an Asian girl who was deaf, Anita was young, white and shy, Jean was a white girl out to make her boyfriend jealous (by checking into the myths about black guys), and Ann was an insecure smoker (more on her later in this chapter). But one of my most memorable love interests occurred when I first arrived in senior high school.

Music was fast becoming a major ingredient in my life, and early in my high school career I decided to join the marching band. We played at the football games as well as the annual homecoming parade. These events also included the participation of an all-girl drill team known as the Highsteppers. Everyone (guys) loved the Highsteppers, with their big smiles and short uniform skirts. And they kept the band looking good also. No matter how bad the football team was doing (and they were often doing badly), everyone loved the sound of the marching band and the look of our field dances, along with the Highsteppers' drill routines.

And that's how I met Rosalyn. She was a year ahead of me, and had already been a member of the Highsteppers for a year. Though I can't remember the exact circumstances of our meeting, I do remember that I became her little buddy in my first year of high school!

She was beautiful to me, with long wavy hair, fair skin, and rather keen features, which appealed to my previously established

28

preferences in women. She stood about 5'9" or

more to my then 6' frame, which made her, in my shyness, out of my league. At the time, she was dating a major player on the football team (isn't that original!), but we often hung out together anyway. I don't know why -- I guess she considered me safe to be around. I often said she showed kindness toward me that she didn't even show her other girlfriends, OR her own boyfriend! And at that time in my life, I really needed someone who esteemed me that much. If it hadn't been for Rosalyn's kindnesses and demeanor, I wasn't far from truly going insane from romantic depression. I remember thinking that if it wasn't for her, I would have easily grown up to be one of those stereotypes you see standing at the asylum window in a bathrobe and slippers, just silently looking out into "whatever" for the rest of my life. Literally! I had been so hurt by my fellow human-beings that I couldn't - or wouldn't - cope anymore. But God knew just what (or *who*) I needed at that point. And through Rosalyn, He *kept me* in the land of sanity. So it's no wonder that there came a time shortly after the holidays when I asked Roz if she would consider being my girlfriend. What a *monumentally bad move* on my part!

First of all, I did it over the phone (too shy for face-to-face); and secondly, I caught her so off-guard that she didn't know how to respond. She wanted to let me down easy, and I don't remember what all she tried telling me, but I was persistent. Finally, I asked if we could at least still be friends, to which she replied "yes" in theory, but in practice she avoided me like the plague! I rarely saw her in school, and she wouldn't return my phone calls. In retrospect, I think she was just afraid of doing or saying anything that might further lead me on. She didn't know that I really wouldn't have done anything more to jeopardize our otherwise great friendship. So instead, I lost the very "light" that had brought me back to the real world from the brink of soulless existence! She eventually graduated and went off to a nearby state university (just out of reach!), never to be seen by me again. If I ever get the opportunity, I would love to let Roz know what a blessing God made her to me at a critical time in my young life.

Another thing I struggled with for the longest time was how God defines "appropriate pursuit." At one point in my younger life, there seemed to be two schools of thought concerning how people got hitched. One line of thought said that your significant-other would appear when you least anticipated it. I had a Christian brother tell me (using Scriptures) that even as Eve was presented to Adam, so Ms. Right would be presented to me in due time, at the right time. He said I just needed to wait and be focused on doing ministry, whatever God had for me to do.

Another line of reasoning said that God made men to be hunter-gatherers, and that "...he who *finds* a wife, finds a good thing" (Proverbs 18:22 NASU). So I needed to be about

30

the business of actively and appropriately seeking Ms. Right for myself (with the Lord's guidance, of course); especially (they said) since women aren't supposed to be initiating such contact in relationships. So there I was, in a "push me, pull you" type of situation; not knowing whether to be patient and wait for some mystery woman to come up beside me, or to get busy searching for the love of my life. Basically, this left me deadlocked in Limbo-land, having neither a girlfriend walking beside me, nor a mate in my sights! And what does the Bible say about a double-minded man (see James 1:7-8)? But after a season or two of being lost in confusion, I decided to try each of the schools of thought.

WAITING

I started with waiting, since that seemed to be the less confrontational of the two schools (remember, I was very shy). I threw my "fishing-line into the water" and myself into occupational opportunities that came my way. Only one nibble had presented itself by the time I was 23, and even that got squelched rather quickly by a step-father with a Napoleon complex. But rather than losing heart, I began to feel that if God was resigning me to lifelong singleness, I just might be able, by His grace, to make it alone. And no sooner had these words come into my brain, than I met "Ann" (not her real name).

Ann was a volunteer worker at one of the many Christian coffeehouses in which I had performed back in those days. She was 21, Caucasian, cute, kind, and ... a smoker. Now I've always been apprehensive about getting involved with someone who smokes, but she seemed genuinely open and interested in me. And since the opportunity presented itself in the process of my doing ministry, I said, "Lord, I owe it to this person, this fellow human-being, and to this potential relationship, to set my prejudices aside long enough to give 'us' a real chance." So we began to date, but I entered into the relationship with both my heart open to love, and my eyes open to the possibility of a severe issue presenting itself at some point. Without getting into all of the gory details, let's just say that there were matters of self-esteem that were taking Ann down from the inside, and they almost took me down with her!

Our relationship started out in an average way, but spiraled into being bad for both of us. For me, I had stopped spending any real quality time with God and my friends, and had really cut down on my church attendance. I had even almost lost my virginity! I don't tell you this story to make a villain out of Ann, but rather to show how, once again, God kept me in spite of my potentially permanent and disastrous decision-making. **It took me four years to undo just the spiritual effects of being in that 8- or 9-month relationship.** Four years to get back to where I <u>was</u> in Christ at the time I met Ann before I could continue my spiritual growth process. And I promised myself I would *never* let something like that happen again!

I continued for many years playing "the Waiting Game," though on occasion I would attempt to go after someone who *really* attracted my eye. Then as I got older, I finally garnered enough guts to actually try *finding* a wife. An example of those efforts is a young woman I'll call "Shaina."

SEEKING/FINDING

I believe Shaina had only become a member of my church a short time before we met. She was a single African-American mom with one son, working a fulltime job while trying to initiate her own business on the side. I was volunteering for a church event this particular year, when I found this very attractive young woman standing nearby me. Somehow I managed to strike up a conversation with her that lasted a good 45 minutes, and included meeting (and being grilled by!) her then 9-year-old son. We exchanged phone numbers, and I attempted to build a relationship/rapport with her. I say "attempted" because as much as I tried to get to know her by calling her on the phone, I could rarely get her to return my calls or initiate her own! We went out on all of two dates (one I paid for, then she insisted on reciprocating), and in the beginning she did tell me of her previous relationships that had gone awry. They had left her in a very tender emotional state. But being the guy that I am, I wanted to take things slow, and show her that I was a better man than those who had misused her.

At first, I thought maybe she was playing some kind of hard-to-get game she learned from *The Rules*[vi,vii] or something. I would call when I was almost positive she was at home, but she never picked up, so I would leave her a message. And when I would see her at church, I wouldn't get more than an obligatory "How are you?" and some lame excuse for not returning my call. I really began to think that she was no longer interested in me, and that she was trying to get me to diminish my interest in her as well.

About that same time, I had been attending a singles' Bible class on being all God created us to be in our singleness, and appropriately seeking out the same in the opposite sex. The class resource book taught that a man should not be so aggressive in his initial romantic pursuit of a woman. Rather he should take his time, get to know her in group situations, and not do ANYTHING that would send false messages to her or give her false expectations. I didn't agree with many of the methods/practices this book put forth, though I did understand its premise; but I was willing to submit to its theories in order to test its validity. What the heck, I was still single after all these years, so obviously I needed *somebody's* help in that department! And I *really* liked Shaina. I continued to be friendly towards her, but I began to back off from my normal tactics of pursuing her.

Well, months of these token interactions and missed calls went by, and I had resigned myself to the idea that we would only be superficial friends, when a notable encounter changed everything! Shaina's birthday had arrived, and I had stopped by her home to wish her a happy birthday, and she was actually there! I found out that none of her family or friends had made any real plans to bless her on her day. So I spontaneously invited her out to dinner, to which she hemmed and hawed for the longest, then finally agreed to go. While at dinner, right out of left field, she asked, "So where do you see this relationship going?" Well, as you may imagine, I was stunned; but remembering her tender psychè, I didn't want to overreact. "Relationship?!", I thought; "What relationship? You, who says little more than 'Boo!' to me at any given time, and refuses to respond to any of my phone calls, you believe we have a relationship . . . that's *going* somewhere?" I tried very hard not to show the shock in my face as I took a bite of my appetizer, but I think I must have failed, because after only a second or two she followed up the question with "...because I'm fine with just being good friends."

God, I truly did like this girl. And I was very attracted to her. But to that point in time, I had kept my emotions in check, while I surveyed the possibilities of romance; and frankly, I had no indications that romance, or even close friendship, was ever going to be possible. She was just too closed-off to me. So I told her that I found her very attractive, but "...I'm not after you." I blamed my non-pursuit on what I was learning from the Bible class I'd been in. She said that she understood, and that we could just be "good friends," but that good friendship never surfaced! From that day forward, Shaina seemed to do everything in her power (though it would be in a concealed way) to hurt me and/or my reputation around the church, even to the point of having the Assistant Pastor feel the need to counsel me about not invading someone's personal space (hers) when communicating with them. Like I had become some kind of stalker or something!

I refused to let her take my joy, and I continued to greet her when I would see her at church, though she worked hard at not acknowledging me as often as she could. I had developed real feelings for her, or at least for who I believed her to be deep down inside. But to my sadness, I had become the very thing that I had worked so hard not to be - another guy who hurt and disappointed Shaina. During that whole Melvin-punishing episode, I saw a side of Shaina that quite frankly, I was glad I hadn't married. Though her situation was one to be pitied, I was not the one who could have come alongside to encourage her. I have some pretty sensitive emotions myself, and God kept me from an emotional pain that was potentially a lot worse than any crisis of singleness I had experienced thus far!

I always kept an eye open that Ms. Right might be standing nearby. But I can count the number of actual girlfriends that I've had in my life on one hand. Generally, if I pursued the women, I was seen either as undesirable (at best), or a stalker (at worst)! And if I waited for her to come my way, I felt like life was passing me by. But there came a point at which I had to ask myself (as one famous psychologist is known to say), "How's that workin' for ya?" And I've gotta say, neither the waiting nor the pursuit strategy was working for me very well! Was keeping women just out of reach part of my Creator's plan on how I was being kept?

V

The Revelations Of 2010

"Thou wilt <u>keep</u> <u>him</u> in perfect peace, whose mind is stayed on <u>Thee</u>…" (Isaiah 26:3)

Two-thousand-ten seemed like just another year-in-the-life at first, but it was to hold some eye-opening and soul-stirring revelations for me. It was time for my mindset to be changed, and like the Christmas ghosts that visited Scrooge, each epiphany built on the wisdom of the previous one.

Revelation One - Own My Age

It started with me quietly hitting my 53rd birthday. I rarely tell folks when my birthday occurs because I hate the inevitable question that follows: "Ooo, how old are you, Melvin?" "Yes" was usually my smiling answer, leaving the inquisitive person with a confused look on their face after several repeated efforts to get a numerical answer from me. My age and my middle name were two questions that I came to hate answering. The latter because I hated my given middle name for psychological reasons; it only got used when I was in trouble with my mom! And the former because being older and <u>never</u> <u>married</u> is *not* something our society deems appropriate to be proud of or comfortable with! But I began to realize that I was reverting to some of my destructive old ways, in that I was letting Life happen *to* me - feeling like a victim under its unstoppable power - rather than me being a victor in Life! So rather than playing the victim to Father Time, I said to myself I needed to take possession of my life and my age. For all of my life (after my early 30s), I felt the need to <u>not</u> reveal my age, especially to females, holding fast to the idea that the women I would be attracted to would not want to give a guy my age the time of day!

But in the Spring of 2010, I started (little by little) telling my true age to certain people - men and women, in various settings - trusting, hoping that it would not run them away or cut short their interest in being my friend (or potential significant-other). I just said to myself, "I've got to begin to be honest with myself and others, and let the chips fall where they may."

<u>REVELATION TWO</u> - Renew My Trust

I remember a particularly poignant conversation I had with some Christian brothers after my singles discussion group one night. My car was broken down at the time, so after the meeting one of the guys offered to take me and a couple of other brothers home via his van. As we went on our way, of course the conversation continued, and I found myself lamenting my age and my singleness to these guys. But the brothers took this opportunity to encourage me to pray about my situation, saying, "If God hasn't taken away these feelings from you all these years, it may be that He wants you to be married...just not right now. It could be that you're not ready, or even *she's* not prepared enough yet." They went on to say that my time would be better spent "being all you can be," all that I'm meant to be, as I wait for the Lord to provide. "Do you <u>trust</u> <u>God</u> for the love you want in your life?" That was an eye-opening moment for me!

That was the real question, wasn't it? That's the underlying thorn in the side of my whole emotional existence. **Do I trust God** in this area of my life? Once I arrived home, I thanked them for their input and encourage-ment, lay on my bed and began to actually meditate on that question, "Do I trust God?" Do I believe He really cares about that area of my life enough for me to give it over to His lordship? Or was it more accurate to admit that I just didn't trust Him with such an important, emotionally gut-wrenching matter? Did I actually feel that He was *keeping me from* romantic happiness because He knew I might love some human more than I loved Him, and He's too jealous of a god to allow that?

I'm embarrassed to admit it, but yes, these thought patterns caused a real struggle in my heart and mind from time to time. But, I ultimately chose to believe John 16:27, that "the Father Himself loves [me]"; and trusting God is something to which I have to renew my dedication regularly!

REVELATION THREE - Realize I Am Kept

I was sharing something along these lines with Rowena, the co-facilitator (at that time) of my co-ed discussion group. In fact, it was the Saturday of the Memorial holiday weekend that year, and we were talking on the phone, basking in the afterglow of our then completed Spring sessions when the conversation somehow turned its focus on me. As I asked Roe about how her dating life was going, she began asking me about how I had gotten so far along in life without having fallen to sexual sin. As I began to bemoan my pitiful condition of never having attracted that kind of attention throughout various situations in my life, Rowena unintentionally helped me to stumble upon a divine truth that had totally eluded me to that point in time. She was amazed that, despite whatever flubs I may have made as a relationship initiator, no female had successfully pursued me either! "It isn't that no one wanted you, Melvin," Roe said, "it's that God kept you. **God really kept you.**" And in that moment, I awoke! I felt the lights turn on.

Ms. Right wasn't being kept just out of reach by a jealous God. I wasn't being taunted by the Devil, nor was I "in my own way!" I wasn't even unattractive. It's just that **I had become a kept man**! Kept by the Lord Who loves me and wants only the best for me within His will.

GOD DESIRES TO KEEP YOU

I am a work in progress, and so are you. The work begins when we surrender ourselves to the One who loves us and created us for Himself, asking Him to come in and take control of our lives. It's vital for us to have and to build a relationship with our Creator/Keeper. I came to understand my need for "fire protection" when I was 12, but it wasn't until I was 17 that I hungered for that deeper relationship! I remember kneeling at the side of my bed on Woodward Avenue and crying out to God for more. "Lord, give me faith. Teach me about faith. There's got to be more to life than this!" And true to His word (see Romans 10:14,17),

The Revelations of 2010

Jesus answered my prayer with knowledge and with His Holy Spirit coming alive inside me. Now my life is about being in a relationship with the One who loves me, created me, and gifted me for a purpose. I desire to use all that I am and all that I have to accurately represent (i.e. glorify) Him in this life. And in spite of my shortcomings, He is committed to me, and is able to do above and beyond what I could ask or think.

He who is perfect in all of His ways wants you to know Him deeply also, just as He already knows you. Jesus expressed this very plainly on several occasions while He was here on earth: "Jesus said to him, Have I been so long with you, and yet you have not come to know Me, Philip? He who has seen Me has seen the Father; so how can you say, 'Show us the Father'?'" (John 14:9 NASU). "And this is eternal life, that they may know You, the only true God, and Jesus Christ whom You have sent" (John 17:3 NASU).

Remember the verse listed at the beginning of the chapter (Isaiah 26:3)? Well there are a ton of others that speak to my (and perhaps your) situation as well. All throughout the Holy Bible are passages that speak of what a mighty God can and will do for those who have chosen to be kept by Him! And it's always better to run **to** God than to run **from** Him because our Keeper is much more interested in healing us of our sins than punishing us for our sins!

    a. "Know that the Lord hath set apart for Himself [him/her] that is godly" (Psalm 4:3).

b. "I know the thoughts I think toward you, says the Lord. Thoughts of peace and not of evil; to give you a future and a hope" (Jeremiah 29:11 NIV).

c. "And we know that God causes all things to work together for good to those who love God, to those who are the called according to His purpose. For those whom He foreknew, He also [preplanned for them] to become conformed to the image of His Son" (Romans 8:28-29 NASU).

d. "Run from sexual immorality! No other sin affects the body as this one does. When you sin this sin it is against your own body. Haven't you yet learned that your body is the home of the Holy Spirit that God gave you?...Your own body does not belong to you. For God has bought you with a great price. So use every part of your body to give [honor] back to God, because he owns it" (1stCorinthians 6:18-20 TLB).

e. "And I am sure that God, Who began this good work within you, will keep right on helping you grow in His grace until His task within you is finally finished" (Philippians 1:6 TLB).

f. "For God is at work within you, helping you want to obey Him, and then helping you do what He wants" (Philippians 2:13 TLB).

g. "Therefore, if anyone will bring their

immorality to an end, they will be a vessel of honor, set apart, fit for the Master's use and prepared for every good work. So run from youthful passions, and instead pursue righteousness, faith, love, and peace, along with those who call on the Lord out of a pure heart" (2nd Timothy 2:21-22) *Author's paraphrase*.

Get Woke, Stay Woke!

The Keeper of the Universe wants to write your life's story! Once you realize **and agree to this** by accepting Him (Jesus) as your Lord and Savior, your amazing narrative will begin to take shape. Open your eyes and your ears to receive instructions on how to live out what He's **preplanned** for you. Because of His love for you, it will all be according to His will and for your best benefit. These days, whenever I feel that Life is happening to me, or in spite of me, I evaluate **if** and **how** God would have **me** respond because, in Life, the only thing we really have any control over is ourselves. I take a moment to pray for understanding and direction. The Lord will let us know in a way that you and I recognize: through His Word, His people, etc. Jesus said, "My sheep **know** My voice and they follow Me" (see John 10:2-4). So then I follow through on (i.e., agree to do) what He says. I am determined to become all I was created to be, and that only happens when I release myself into His hands by **obeying** His Spirit within me -- as soon as He speaks!

Now I'll be the first to say that being kept this way may not always be enjoyable...or appreciated. Even though in our heart of hearts we should know that our celibacy is God's will and in our best interest, at times we may still feel neglected, marginalized, or unseen. And we'll want to take matters into our own hands! Though our best-laid plans for "happiness" may leave others sorely impacted in the aftermath, it still somehow feels justifiable to take control, if only because "Surely the God Who loves me doesn't want me to suffer [loneliness, cupidity, depression, etc.] like this!" For many of us unmarried individuals, we have bought into the subtle yet erroneous propaganda that a complete and fulfilled life should by definition include marriage, or some form of committed coupling. But contrary to "The Hype," marriage is not the be-all and end-all of life!

To explain it as simply as possible, we are conditioned from an early age to feel that a life is less lived if a marriage doesn't occur in it. The message comes through endless informational outlets, such as the Media (film and TV shows, commercials, magazine articles, etc.), our families and peers, and unwittingly even from many of our places of worship. It's the American Dream: get an education, start a career, GET MARRIED, buy a house and car, have kids, pay your bills and taxes, and drive your retirement RV into the sunset. Arguably, the images and information it conveys, coupled with our natural instinct to have sex, create and then feed our never-ending quest to link up with the opposite sex in a monogamous, committed relationship (whether that's getting married or some "other arrangement"). Subsequently, when this pairing doesn't occur in a timely fashion (according to *our* time clock), depression and angst build. Self-doubt and low self-esteem can set in. And we blame God. This encourages poor decision-making and more reckless behavior on our part. We say, "If God won't make it happen, then I must!" And promiscuity proliferates, men get misogynistic, women are wounded, alternative lifestyles are attempted, and divorces are destined; all because our focus gets flawed.

I know I was well into my middle-aged years before I realized how flawed my thinking was. I had bought into The Hype. And because I hadn't married in a timely fashion (according to its tenets), I subconsciously couldn't continue its process, the life cycle, the American Dream. Until I did get married, there would be no need to buy a house, and it would be inappropriate to have kids. By necessity I had to pay my bills, but my sunset retirement was not planned out nor looking too pretty. I was stuck living in that *pre-marriage* season of life, like a damaged CD continuing to skip backwards in the song by a half-second. And psychologically, it became important to me to maintain a public persona of a man in his prime until I had successfully accomplished that marriage piece. That's why, amongst other flawed reasoning and behavior, one of my biggest was my attraction to women in their 30s (when I was hitting my 50s!), and that's why I never revealed my age. I wasn't trusting the Lord to get me married, and I didn't realize I was being kept.

But why set aside God's perfect handiwork in our daily lives to function in our own wisdom and strength (Proverbs 12:15 and 14:12-14)? It pays to remember that it's Love who is caring for our future, just like He said He cares about every hair on our head (Luke 21:15-18). Love knows what things we have need of *before* we even ask for them (Matthew 6:8), and Love covers many of our missteps and bad choices along the way (1st Peter 4:8). He's the one Who's written the perfect life story, just for you, and it's waiting to be revealed through you. **Don't resist it!**

VI

Becoming A Kept Person

My life has significantly changed since the revelations of 2010. My priorities have shifted and my pursuits have realigned. I am now more concerned with:

a. my calling(s) — I've made a point of *learning* my gifts and callings in order to pursue them consciously and diligently. Our Creator was intentional about how He gifted me and the purposes for which He designed me. It only makes sense that I should be intentional about discovering those gifts and callings and diligent about using them for the sake of the world around me.

b. my relationships — On whom should I utilize my gifts and callings more but those closest to me? Who better to receive what I have to offer than my friends and family? You and I are blessed to be a blessing to those around us, especially those we connect with on a regular basis (Galatians 6:10).

c. my essential mentoring connections -- All of us are called to pass on any wisdom that we gain during our life, especially godly wisdom (Deuteronomy 6:5-9).

Jesus was a great example of these three pursuits during His own earthly life. He immersed Himself in His calling to reach those uninformed about the coming Kingdom. He valued and blessed His family and close friendships with empathy, compassionate deeds, wise counsel, and tough love when necessary, successfully mentoring more than a few men and women in the process. **And He was *never* married.** Yes, I've discovered that what can be had in romantic relationships can also be found in good friendships that you establish with <u>both</u> genders, minus the sexual contact of course, even as Jesus did.[viii] I *personally* experienced this when I lived in Nashville in the early '90s.

In addition to being a multi-college town, Nashville was becoming a mecca for Christian music and its young musical wannabes. Because many of its citizens were transplants from other cities, it was very easy to make new friends and get involved with fun social activities. Besides the natural southern hospitality that existed, new arrivals were automatically more socially "open" because, if you weren't, you had no one else. It was my first time living away from Cleveland for any extended period of time. And while there, I attended one of the hottest churches in (what they called) "the Nashville circuit." It was one of "the" churches for many of Christian music's elite, boasting a membership of thousands, with a median age of 31, and more than 40% of the congregation being unmarried. And it was in this setting that I met great friends. I had friends for activities, friends for making music together, and friends for great conversation. There wasn't a day that went by (notice, I didn't just say "weekend!") where there wasn't something fun or interactive to enjoy with my peers, whether it was listening to a lounge band, participating in ultimate frisbee at a park, playing indoor volleyball, eating at a restaurant, or just visiting from house to house. I was actually living out what some only viewed on TV shows like *Thirtysomething*[ix] or *Friends*.[x]

Sharing in positive social events and interactions creates lasting memories. Deep conversations about meaningful issues build bonds of relational intimacy, where loyalty and trust can grow great friendships that last a lifetime. This keeps us learning and growing personally, and allows our Keeper to have an impact on the people in our world through us! Truth be told, I'm really in the process of learning how ANY relationship is built and maintained. My history of dysfunctional interactions didn't train me for building healthy relationships with people. But God used Nashville to train and improve me in the area of interpersonal skills, and I'm trusting Him Who began this good work in me to see it through to completion (Philippians 1:6). So, though I experienced a lack of hugs and kisses in my childhood, God was setting up for me the importance of physical touch in my future relationships (John 13:23). When I was being bullied by everyone around me, God was preparing me to be a soft-hearted listener and helper to other down-trodden individuals around me (2nd Corinthians 1:3-4 NIV). When I was way too shy around the opposite sex, that was one way the Lord kept me abstinent. When my self-esteem was very low and I thought I was being kept from true love, when the countless women I pursued or was attracted to were kept just out of reach, that was actually my Heavenly Father

<u>keeping</u> <u>me</u> from misplaced attractions and unhealthy/ungodly relationships (Psalm 141:3-4). Meanwhile, I continued to vigorously pursue my purpose in life by learning my design, my giftedness, and my calling.

THE TOOLS FOR PURPOSEFUL LIVING

The first thing that contributed to my pursuit-of-purpose was learning about my God-given design through a study program called The Career Kit.[xi] Though it's no longer published today, The Kit was a collection of six workbooks that walked the reader through an understanding of God's purpose for work in the life of every individual, and how to discover one's own career path. It covered everything, from paying attention to your passions, setting career goals and salary expectations, how to interview, and even continuing your lifework into retirement. It helped me to recognize that I had already been operating in my design and skill set before I even became aware of what my inate abilities were! It helped me to understand the importance of pursuing the right kind of jobs for which I am suited, that work is meant to be a joy and not a punishment, and that my paycheck can feel like a fringe benefit instead of a struggle. It took a few months to process through all the material but I still make use of many of its principles and practices to this day. What is it that occupies your time and thoughts throughout the day? What do you do well, whether for pay or for free, that's so exciting to you and perhaps beneficial to others that you'd rather keep doing it than to break for dinner or sleep? The answer to questions like these is a clue to your true design. And knowing how your Creator designed you is essential to living in your purpose.

Another helpful item for pursuing my purpose was taking an inventory of my gifts. The Bible tells us that our natural abilities (craftsmanship, critical thinking, athletics, etc.) are installed at birth (e.g., Genesis 4:20-22) and are developed through use and experience; but everyone who gives themselves to God's keeping (i.e. becomes a Christian) is also given at least one *spiritual* gift as well (1st Corinthians 12:1-11). And our Keeper wants everyone to understand their giftedness. Assessments, coupled with good biblical teaching, help us determine more clearly what gifts we've been given and how to operate in them appropriately. These gifts are intended to help us navigate the world around us, and be a blessing to others. To understand my gifts, both natural and spiritual, I participated in several classes and evaluations offered by my church and others over the years (It was also my church that had invested in the purchase of the Career Kit that I used). There are three assessments that I'd like to recommend to you here:

a) S.H.A.P.E.[xii] This in-depth guide (from the folks who brought us *The Purpose-Driven Life*) can be found on numerous church websites or ordered through bookstores. The acronym stands for spiritual gifts, heart, abilities, personality, and experiences; and through this material you can learn what your passions, skills, gifts and temperament are, and how they work together to help you find and fulfill your unique purpose in life.

b) <u>LifeKeys</u>[xiii]-This guidebook helps you understand, evaluate, and apply your gifts, values, passions, and personality to discover (as their subtitle suggests) "who you are, why you're here, and what you do best." Through examination of these, you are better able to pinpoint your God-given place and purpose in life.

c) <u>Spiritual Gifts Assessment</u>[xiv] – This is an online, comprehensive dive into discovering your biblical, spritual gifts. Through the analysis of your responses to 108 questions/statements, it will reveal your dominant spiritual gift(s) and teach you how they operate. Then, with your eyes wide open, your Creator can develop and exercise them in your daily life. This questionnaire can be found at <gifts.churchgrowth.org/spiritual-gifts-survey>; produced by The Team Ministry.

A third tool in my pursuit of purpose was being aware of my Keeper's calling on my life. It's only recently (actually, since the beginning of writing this book!) that I've realized how long and how far away I've been from my true mandate. As I said earlier, we can't help but function in our God-given design, even early in our lives before we understand the concepts of design or purpose. For me, my primary calling (to encourage others through the written word) started with finding my voice through poetry, and as I grew in my Christianity, it moved into the arenas of songwriting and sending out letters of encouragement. But somehow it eventually morphed into just drafting legal documents for myself and others. Somewhere, in the process of living, I got away from my calling. Though many folks saw that I had a knack for writing, I somehow lost the motivation to use that skill to aid others. . .until now.

THE TURN OF THE PAGE

The intentionality of my current journey was actually something that I had begun back in April of 2008, after the eye-opening insight I received while on sabbatical that year. You see, I have had a habit in recent years of going on an annual retreat somewhere to get alone with God, and taking some sort of self-help or self-improvement reading with me. That year, it was Myles Munroe's *In Pursuit of Purpose.*[xv] It proved to be a very inspiring book, one that helped me focus on my personal pursuit of my divine destiny. In the process of all that I learned from it, one eye-opener was that whenever the purpose for something created is not initially recognized, there's a danger of misuse, or waste, or even permanent loss because you don't know how to effectively employ that invention in its intended purpose. And I made a note to myself that it is important and helpful for me to not move ahead on significant matters (e.g., marriage, schooling, jobs, etc.) without a sense of knowing God's intention or purpose for the said decision/event to occur!

Not that we're guaranteed to understand everything about any one situation in life, but it's important to not just walk through life

Becoming A Kept Person

blindly, never seeking clarity of purpose for the things that are pursued or the choices that are made. That's what I used to do: just let Life happen to me. That's how I used to respond to Life's ups and downs. But now I understand that God created me (and you) with a definite calling and purpose in mind. And I want to live up to it! My very existence is evidence that this generation needs something that my life contains, that my presence is necessary, and that my purpose needs to be fulfilled. And this is true of you too!

Haven't you and I been slowed down and sidetracked long enough by the wrong pursuits? Our Adversary, the Devil, would have us remain distracted by:

1. *a painful past* – There are so many things that I have done for love, or done to be in love. Embarrassing things. Unnecessary things. And none of it got me any closer to what I wanted or where I believed I belonged. It only left me with feelings of shame, worthlessness, and desperation.

2. *our current sin* – How can I be an effective representative of my Creator if I'm only focused on fighting (or feeding) my flesh? Always concentrating on fixing our sin takes our eyes off of being His light in a dark world (Matthew 5:16). We do have to confess and forsake our sins but that's not our main mission!

3. *any ongoing circumstances* – These may include financial instability, a perceived poor or weak status in life, and/or other relational inhibitors. For me, romantic

54

happiness through marriage has been elusive so far. And yet I cannot let this define my existence any longer. And neither should you!

My Keeper called me out of a painful past to be/pursue who I was created to be: "I cried to You, O Lord; oh, how I pled!...Then He turned my sorrow into joy! He took away my clothes of mourning and clothed me with joy, so that I might sing glad praises to the Lord instead of lying in silence in the grave. O Lord my God, I will keep on thanking You forever!" (Ps 30:8,11-12 TLB); also the apostle Peter reminds us, "You have been chosen by God Himself - you are priests of the King, you are holy and pure, you are God's very own - all this so that you may show to others how God called you out of the darkness into His wonderful light. Once you were less than nothing; now you are God's own. Once you knew very little of God's kindness; now your very lives have been changed by it." (1st Peter 2:9-10 TLB)

Though resisting the motivation to sin may seem noble and appropriate, what I've learned is "Don't fight the flesh, **feed the spirit.**" It's a phrase we came up with years ago in a men's Bible study group I attended. It's about not putting all our efforts into fighting our sin nature, but rather spending time learning and growing in God! Why go down fighting defensively against sin when you can stand up and keep moving **proactively** towards righteousness and fulfilled potential? Old immoral attitudes and activities will pass away as your new character grows (2nd Corinthians

5:17). It's the old saying of "which dog you feed wins the fight!"

And as for our ongoing circumstances, our main priority from now on should be to "Seek **first** the kingdom of God and His righteousness" (Matthew 6:33 NIV). When we are going about our Heavenly Father's business there's no time for feeling sorry for ourselves or for getting sappy about our circumstances! There's no room for the Devil to have a "field day" in our minds. Kingdom virtues are about the pursuit of pleasing our Creator, and helping others, more than satisfying ourselves. When we recognize that we're kept by God to fulfill His purposes, we're less concerned about what we do or don't have, knowing that our Keeper knows what things we need before we even ask for them (Matthew 6:8).

I want to share something I wrote when I was in my mid-twenties. This modern-day psalm was written/adapted while I was in the midst of feeling abandoned in my loneliness, banished by God to singlehood (like it was a bad thing!). I had no girlfriend, so I longed to recognize and regularly experience deep intimacy with the God who said He loves me. During that time, I had searched out the reference text of my favorite hymn, "Great Is Thy Faithfulness" (Lamentations 3:21-32a), and while I read it, my soul began to connect with the choice of words I found there. As I began to study and meditate on this portion of scripture, I think the cross-references sent me to the book of Micah as well (see Micah 7:7-9). Together, they really "spoke" what my heart was feeling (and what I wanted my heart to feel!) in that season of my life. May you find

Becoming A Kept Person

comfort and a voice from them as well...and say "yes" to becoming a kept man/woman!

Twigg's Psalm[xvi]

1 *The Lord is my portion, saith my soul: in Him is all my substance.*

2 *The Lord is my portion; without Him, I would fail.*

3 *The Lord is my high tower, outside of Him there is no Life.*

4 *My God is Jehovah, the source of all good things.*

5 *Jehovah is my provider, in Him I must trust; but blest is the man whose God is the Lord!*

6 *This I recall to my mind, and therefore have I hope. It is because of the Lord's mercies that I am not consumed! Because His compassions never fail.*

7 *They are new every morning; great is His faithfulness.*

8 *So, the Lord is my portion, saith my soul; therefore will I hope in Him.*

Selah (musical pause for thought)

9 *The Lord is good unto those that wait for Him, to the soul that diligently seeks Him.*

10 *It is good that a man should both hope and quietly wait for the salvation of the Lord.*

11 *Therefore I will look unto the Lord; I will wait for the God of my salvation. My God will hear me.*

12 *Rejoice not against me, O my enemy; for when I fall, I shall arise. When I sit in darkness, the Lord shall be a light unto me.*

13 *I will bear this indignation of the Lord, because I have sinned against Him; until Jesus pleads my cause, and executes judgment for me!*

14 *He will bring me forth to the light, and I shall behold His righteousness!*

VII

The Journey Continues

So I've turned a page. And I've changed my focus. I'm tired of being stagnant, sad, or bitter. I'm **pursuing my potential** rather than pursuing a mate! If she comes, she comes. I'll see her; my Keeper will make sure of it because it will be in His will and in His timing. He'll certainly be able to convince me when she's the one. Along the way, I have to keep trusting that God is guiding me in His pathways and protecting me from hurt, harm and danger...and even from myself! I say especially from myself because oftentimes I (we!) can be my (our) own worst enemy. My plans often fail when they don't have the Lord's ends in mind. I've learned about (and continue to improve at) hearing and obeying that still, small Voice spoken of in 1st Kings 19:12-13. It's the prompting of the Lord's Spirit in the quieted center of my mind. When I listen for and follow *that* guidance, then *appropriate* plans are made...and accomplished (Proverbs 16:9). And I remain A KEPT MAN.

My story is still being written. It began with my feeling unloved and unwanted, and not learning how to appropriately interact with the opposite sex. Through my human eyes, I felt unsupported, unattractive, and bullied. And I couldn't understand what was wrong with me, that love and romance constantly eluded me. But from a heavenly perspective, all that I've been through shows how and why I'm actually a kept man. God threw out a "lifeline" in every situation, as He promises He will (1st Corinthians 10:13 NASU), starting with the kindnesses of His people (e.g., Rev. Hill, Rosalyn, and others). He continued by educating me in His values and His ways, and training me in interpersonal skills, such as during my time in Nashville. But along the way I also grew to understand my design and giftedness, and how to better pursue my purpose in life. We can't forget the revelations of 2010, of owning my age, trusting God more, and *realizing* I am a kept man. Of course, my obedience to His guidance had to change, and my priorities have narrowed to focus on my callings as well as my primary and mentoring relationships. These things now provide me with joy in the journey of life rather than the disillusion I felt about "missing" my *expected* destination. All of this took place contrary to the so-called Cycle of Life, but it was all in God's master plan because my Creator loves me and has a divine manuscript for my life.

Throughout the Word of God, there are numerous examples of individuals and groups of people being **kept** by our Creator in one way or another:

a. Even after their sin of disobedience, God protected Adam & Eve from the elements by personally clothing them (Genesis 3:21)!

b. *He* closed the hatch on the Ark, to keep Noah's family and the animals alive & afloat during the Flood (Genesis 7:16).

c. God kept the prophet Elijah from starvation and execution (1st Kings 17 and 18).

The Journey Continues

d. Our Heavenly Father <u>kept</u> Job from being killed by Satan, and even replaced the family and property he originally lost (Job 1 and 42:10-17).

e. Jonah was <u>set</u> <u>apart</u> to deliver God's proclamation, and even though he initially resisted, he completed the mission and the Lord <u>attended</u> <u>to</u> his physical needs (Jonah 1-4).

f. Mother Mary was <u>kept</u> innocent by God, in order to fulfill the requirement for Jesus' birth. The Creator dictated that our guilt for sin can only be washed away by the blood of a spotless sacrifice. The Lamb of God (Jesus) had to be born of a <u>virgin</u> in order to be "stain-free" of Man's sinfulness until the appropriate time [His sacrificial death on the cross] (Matthew 1:23-25; Luke 1:26-35; John 1:29).

g. Jesus Himself was <u>kept</u> from being arrested or stoned to death on several occasions (Matthew 21:45-46; Luke 4:28-30; John 8:57-59 and John 10:30-39); then He <u>kept</u> the first disciples unified and growing (John 17:11-17).

All of this divine maintenance in the lives of kept people occurs regardless of what their romantic or marital status is or will be! So now, I believe *if* I am being kept for a future significant-other, she will present herself at the right time, and in the right place. What I've come to understand about romantic endeavors is that the best way to find Mr./Ms. Right requires both waiting <u>and</u> pursuit! Not a lifeless plopping down on a couch somewhere, hoping our paths might cross someday, but **active waiting**: being busy about our Heavenly Father's business and our pursuit of His purpose for our lives. Being active in one's career and obedient to one's calling/ministry. Then, **pursuit** comes in the form of placing ourselves in the right environments to *find or be found by* him/her, praying for God to open our eyes and heart to *see* him/her, and then when (s)he is revealed, being confident and honest enough to *tell* him/her of our attraction. Just like Adam and Eve, it will be/feel natural - for both of us.

But I also now understand and believe that if I **never marry**, my life should be nonetheless full of purpose and meaning, with many joys and few regrets, because **life is about becoming**. Most importantly, it's about becoming a close companion to our divine Keeper. And then becoming all that He created us to be. He is *always* our significant-other. . . our most Significant-Other.

I am a senior citizen who has never had sex and has never been married...and it's okay. In fact, it's more than okay, it's perfect because I have been kept by God. His work is perfect, and all His ways are right (Deuteronomy 32:4). There are still occasional struggles with self-esteem, lust, temptation, and other faulty thoughts and behaviors, because I am still in this imperfect body (1st Corinthians 15:53). Our Creator didn't promise us a struggle-free life; instead He offers us His comfort, presence, and help **through** those life-struggles (2nd Corinthians 12:9-10 TLB). That's the Promise; that in peace God will **keep** those whose mind is stayed on Him, those who trust Him (Isaiah 26:3-4).

61

The Journey Continues

There is great gain in being kept by God. Being single and celibate in life is not the horrible, social "death row" that some segments of society and Media would make it out to be. And it's not a failure on your part. Stop telling yourself that! And stop listening to those who make you feel that way. Like me, it may have nothing to do with your choices in partners, or your shyness in romance. But rather, you are just a KEPT person. Don't let former negative thought patterns (e.g., The Hype) continue to play in your mind. Celibacy is an achievement! It's an accomplishment that more and more people of all ages are ascribing to AND attaining. Maybe even folks YOU know. Notable folks like Olympian and track star Lori "LoLo" Jones who in her thirties has openly proclaimed her virginity; NFL quarterback Tim Tebow who, being raised by Baptist missionary parents, is waiting until he's married before having sex; and Grammy-nominated, Dove award-winning singer/song-writer Jamie Grace ("Do Life Big" and "Hold Me"), who's been credited with this great statement: "I believe I was created by the Creator of Love. And it's my goal to live a life...doing whatever it is He has in store [for me] while I am, and *after I have*, waited for the love of my life...and I really hope that you'll give waiting a chance too." [xvii]

But even not-so-famous people are recognizing the value of abstinence, like Krista, a single in her late thirties, who's made the decision to wait until marriage: "I come from a home where sex was spoken of as natural, exciting, and totally important...within

The Journey Continues

marriage!" And there's Emily, who made her decision to remain abstinent-until-marriage when she was still a young teenager, and says that celibacy is the second-best decision of her life. And one man's anonymous declaration was, "My wife and I believe that sex is a spiritual experience. We waited until marriage to have sex, and we could not have been happier. I know that most people would judge us as religious nut-jobs and whatnot, but we chose to believe that there's more to sex than the physical experience. We believe that for us humans there should also be the emotional element, which elevates the experience to something more special."

About 3% of Americans successfully wait until marriage to have sex, which may seem like a small number, but that represents nearly 10,000,000 successful waiters. That's ten million people (alive right now, in the US alone) who waited, found love, got married, <u>then</u> had sex for the first time. Also, in the general population, the ratio of women-to-men who wait until marriage to have sex seems to be about 60/40 girls-to-guys. This statistic disproves the common misconception that only women wait until marriage to have sex. Statistically-speaking, plenty of guys wait too! [xviii]

Virginity-until-marriage is not only a safer and healthier way of life, it's a godly prerequisite (1st Corinthians 7:8-9). And singleness is a divine gift. The ability to:

a) make independent decisions,
b) be spontaneous with little restriction,

and

c) find and pursue your God-given passions and goals <u>without</u> <u>distraction</u>

are all facets of this gift. In fact, it's one of the first gifts we <u>all</u> receive. **Do you realize** we are ALL born into this world as an <u>unmarried</u> <u>virgin</u>?! It is by Divine design. As I said in the preface, what I am in life is directly due to being in the grip of my Keeper as I grew up and matured; and, I might add here, how I *responded* to His work in my life.

Our Creator promised in His word that **"all things work together for the good** to those that love God and are the called according to His purpose" (Romans 8:28). My pastor recently explained it this way: "God knows what's best for you! And God causes all things to *work together* [for our good]. And He's working on your situation. You say, 'Even tough stuff?' Yeah. 'Even bad stuff?' Yes. 'Even unfair stuff?' Yeah. It may not seem like it at face value, when you're going through it...that news from the doctor...the date that was turned down...that job you lost unexpectedly. But think about it like this. When you make a cake, the independent ingredients may not taste that good. Baking soda doesn't taste that good by itself. Salt [or flour!] doesn't taste that good by itself. So along the way, we have some ingredients that don't play well by themselves. But God is *working* ALL THINGS *together*; you give it time...", and they become a baked item that's savory to the taste!

So through human eyes, your abstinence may not feel like a good place for you to be right now. There may have been times when

The Journey Continues

your unmarried status didn't look right or "taste good." Yet your singleness may not be an uncalled-for situation. You're being KEPT to accomplish great works by He who is your <u>first love</u>; so submit to it! If you're reading this book and happen to unintentionally be an unmarried, celibate person, don't consider your position to have just come from blind fate or unfortunate circumstances. You may need to realize, just as I had to, that you too are being kept by God! It's appropriate to be at this place in your life. And you need to positively receive from and respond to the One who loves you and brought you to this point.

> Come unto Me, all you who labor and are [over-burdened], and I will give you rest. Take My yoke [i.e., connecting clamp] upon you, and learn [about] Me, for I am meek and lowly in heart, and you shall find rest for your souls. For My yoke is easy and My burden is light.
>
> –Jesus Christ,
> Matthew 11:28-30

So, will you pursue who you're DESTINED to be? Will you do what you're CALLED to do? You, my friend, are intended to become a kept person. You may not know it yet, but your season of singleness and celibacy can turn out to be more emotionally and spiritually fulfilling than any marriage you've ever seen or imagined; so embrace it! Be CAUGHT UP with your Creator/Keeper. And the God of grace WILL take care of you.

ENDNOTES

Preface
[i]"What You Are Is Where You Were When" is a video hosted by Morris E. Massey. Magnetic Video Corp., 1976.

Chapter 3
[ii]Latchkey kid (1944): a young child of working parents who must spend part of their day unsupervised (as at home). The term is derived from the need to give the child a key to get in/out of their house on their own. (see *Merriam-Webster's Collegiate Dictionary-10th Ed.*)
[iii]Twigg. "That's The Way I Am With Love." Melvin Mason, 1975.
[iv]Later changed to "...a grim view, of me an older man with nothing to do."

Chapter 4
[v]Twigg. Excerpt of a poem, title unknown. Melvin Mason, circa 1974.
[vi]Fein, Ellen; Sherrie Schneider. *The Rules: Time-tested Secrets for Capturing the Heart of Mr. Right*. Warner Books, 1995.
[vii]NOTE: *There were many experts and laymen at the time of its publication who felt that the principles and processes outlined in* The Rules *were significantly irrational and unreasonable for use in contemporary society.*

Chapter 6
[viii]Scriptures that show Jesus' friendships include Luke 7:34-36, 10:38-42, John 11:1-45, 12:1-2, 13:23-24, and 21:7-12, all in TLB.

[ix]*Thirtysomething* was a TV drama series about the anxiety and insecurities felt by baby boomers & yuppies in the United States as depicted through the interactions of 3 young urban couples and their related friends. The show ran from 1987 to 1991.

[x]*Friends* was a TV sitcom series revolving around the ups and downs in the lives of six single friends in their 20s and 30s who live in Manhattan. The show ran from 1994 to 2004.

[xi]Staub, Dick; Jeff Trautman. *Intercristo's Career Kit: A Christian's Guide to Career Building*. Intercristo, 1985, 1986.

[xii]Rees, Erik. *S.H.A.P.E.: Finding and Fulfilling Your Unique Purpose for Life*. Zondervan Publishing House, 2008.

[xiii]Kise, Jane A. G.; David Stark; Sandra Krebs Hirsh. *LifeKeys: Discovering Who You Are, Why You're Here, What You Do Best*. Bethany House Publishers, 1996.

[xiv]Gilbert, Larry. *Spiritual Gifts Survey*. ChurchGrowth.org, 2014.

[xv]Munroe, Myles. *In Pursuit Of Purpose*. Destiny Image Publishers, 1992.

[xvi]Mason, Melvin. "Twigg's Psalm," from the album *Music In My Heart*. Twigg Productions, 1985.

Chapter 7

[xvii]Grace, Jamie. "Boys, Boys, Boys." *YouTube*, YouTube, 15 Feb. 2013, <youtu.be/h3865 MHq6Z4>. To hear more from Jamie, go to <youtu.be/bEW0tO6JhVc>.

[xviii]Mike. "4 Cool Statistics About Abstinence in the USA." *WaitingTillMarriage.org*, 30 Nov. 2012, <waitingtillmarriage.org/4-cool-statistics-about-abstinence-in-the-usa/>.

Made in the USA
Coppell, TX
16 May 2021